SPEECH[illegible]

—OF—

JOHN A. ANDREW

—AT—

HINGHAM AND BOSTON,

TOGETHER WITH

HIS TESTIMONY BEFORE THE HARPER'S FERRY COMMITTEE

OF THE SENATE, IN RELATION TO

JOHN BROWN.

—ALSO—

THE REPUBLICAN PLATFORM

AND OTHER MATTERS.

PUBLISHED BY ORDER OF THE REPUBLICAN STATE COMMITTEE.

Reception at Hingham.

John A. Andrew among His Towns-People.

A CORDIAL "WELCOME HOME."

Phonographically Reported for the Traveller by J. M. W. Yerrinton.

JOHN A. ANDREW, Esq., the Republican nominee for Governor, resides, during the summer months, in the fine old town of Hingham, down by the sea-shore, where he has made his home for some years. On Saturday, he returned there from most effective and noble service in the canvass now so energetically prosecuted in Maine, and his fellow-townsmen, irrespective of party affiliation, determined to give him a reception which should testify their admiration and love for the man, and their conviction that his nomination by the Republican party, as their candidate for the chief office in the gift of the Commonwealth, was one eminently "fit to be made." The time fixed was Monday evening, Sept. 3d, and notwithstanding the brief notice that could be given (for the preparations were, almost literally, the work of an hour), the demonstration was not only large in point of numbers, but most hearty and enthusiastic in its character, and must have been exceedingly gratifying to the genial and warm-hearted gentleman in whose honor it was conceived and carried out.

At eight o'clock, several hundred people gathered in front of Loring's Hall, where they were marshalled in procession, and, preceded by the North Weymouth Band, marched through the streets of the beautiful and ancient town, the way being illuminated by the blaze of blue lights and the flash of rockets, and the air stirred with the frequent cheers of the rejoicing multitude. The good people of Hingham seemed to be all astir, and balcony, door-way and window were thronged with eager and happy faces, while groups were gathered in the streets at the most available positions, who greeted the procession as it passed with cheers and shouts. Many buildings were illuminated, and every thing was lively and animated as upon a holiday.

About nine o'clock, the march ended, for the time, in front of Mr. Andrew's house, where a large company had already assembled, in anticipation of the arrival of the procession. Among the number were many gentlemen not of Mr. Andrew's household of political faith, who took part in the festivities of the occasion with heartiness and zeal. The fair ladies of the town were present, in large numbers, and thronged the garden in front of the house, giving an added loveliness to the scene.

Arrived at the house, the band played "Hail to the Chief," after which the crowd made the welkin ring with three cheers for Mr. Andrew. T. T.

Bouvé, Esq., then addressed the assembly as follows:—

Speech of T. T. Bouve, Esq.

GENTLEMEN,—We come together in response to a call made upon us, without distinction of party I trust and hope, to do honor to our friend and neighbor, JOHN A. ANDREW, by expressing to him, in our gathering together, in our hearty plaudits, and in the few words we can utter, the deep feelings of respect, of admiration and of love that move our hearts toward him.

It seems a fitting occasion, now that one of the great parties of the State has nominated him as its representative man, that, differing though we may in politics, we should come forward and congratulate him together upon this great compliment to his talents and manly worth. It is a compliment of which any man may justly feel proud, and knowing JOHN A. ANDREW as we do, we certainly all unite in the feeling that the party has done itself honor in nominating such a man.

I am sure that it is not necessary here to dwell upon the characteristics that distinguish our friend; I am sure that he is too well known to you; and I, therefore, without further remark, introduce to you JOHN A. ANDREW, ESQ.

Nine hearty cheers were given for Mr. Andrew, the band played a lively strain, and then the distinguished gentleman addressed his town's-people as follows:

Speech of John A. Andrew, Esq.

Mr. Bouve, and Friends and Neighbors of the goodly and ancient town of Hingham:—This is one of those occasions which occur sometimes in the course of all our lives, when no poor form of human speech is adequate, either to the solemnity or to the gladness of the hour. I confess to you, my old friends and neighbors, associates and kinspeople of the town of Hingham, that I could fitter speak by tears than speak by voice or word tonight. From the centre of my being, from the bottom of my heart, for this unsought, enthusiastic and cordial welcome, this tender of your generous sympathies, in a moment most important and significant in my private or public humble career, I can only say, dear friends I thank you.

I am not here to-night, as it is sometimes my lot to be, addressing an assembly of my fellow-citizens upon matters of public concernment, touching which they and I may either agree or differ; for I understand—and this thought lends both sweetness and pathos to the emotions of the hour—I am here to-night among neighbors and friends, who, for the moment, are all agreed to differ, and all consenting to agree. In all the exigencies of our private or our public fortunes, we mean—we of Hingham, we of this old Puritan commonwealth, peopled by intelligent, faithful, pious and progressive minds and hearts—we mean to be faithful to the sacred duties and cares of friendship. As my private friends, not as public associates, not as political coadjutors, I now gladly receive your greetings and your sympathies; and again, dear friends, I repeat that my heart leaps in unspoken and unspeakable words of grateful joy to receive this homage of your sympathy and love. (Loud applause.)

How dear to my heart are these fields, these hills, these spreading trees, this verdant grass, this sounding shore before you, where, now, for fourteen years, through summer heat, and sometimes through winter storms, I have trod your streets, rambled through your woods, sauntered by your shores, sat by your firesides, and felt the warm pressure of your hands; sometimes teaching your children in the Sunday school, sometimes speaking to my fellow-citizens—always with the cordial friendship of those who differed from me oftentimes in what they thought the radicalism of my opinions—speaking to willing ears,—very much more willing to hear than my words were worthy to be listened to,—on topics most interesting to your minds and convictions. Here—*here* I have found most truly a home of the soul, free from the cares and distractions, from the turmoil and doubts and anxieties and responsibilities of a careful and anxious profession. Away from the busier haunts of men, it has been given to me here to find a calm and sweet retreat, where, in the love of those who have given to me the boon of private friendship, I have been able to refresh the harrassed and wearied spirit, and strengthen the worn and tottering frame. Here, too, dear friends, I have found the home of my heart. It was into one of your families that I entered, and joined myself in holy bonds of domestic love to one of the daughters of your town. (Hearty cheers.) Here, too, have I first known a parent's joys and a parent's sorrows. But it is not for me, nor is this the moment, to enlarge upon, or detail, thoughts which come too near to any man to be spoken in words.

I have, my dear friends and neighbors, as your mouthpiece and representative tonight has so kindly mentioned, been selected by one of the great parties of the Commonwealth of Massachusetts, to bear their standard in the approaching political campaign. For that honor I am to thank others, not the people of Hingham alone; for that responsibility I am indebted to others, not solely, certainly, to you. But it is because it has fallen to me to stand in a position which may lead me, at some early day, to occupy a chief seat in the places of power, that you have come here this evening to say to me, that whether here or there, you are still my friends. (Prolonged applause.) And I have dared to present myself here, and to lift up my voice, and to say, with all the earnestness and honestness of a manly conviction, that whether you say Aye or No to that selection, John A. Andrew is for ever your friend. (Enthusiastic applause, with three cheers.)

A certain sturdy honesty and independence of purpose have from the first distinguished the people of Hingham,—from the first have distinguished the people of this old pilgrim colony, of which your beautiful and historic town forms a part. I remember an illustration of this in the story of your town, written by a distinguished native of your soil. The first minister who dispensed the Word of God in that venerable and commodious structure consecrated to His service, now the oldest, I believe, in which his word is preached in the Union, when, in the year 1647, the people of Hingham chose to set up for themselves an opinion concerning a matter interesting and pertinent to their municipal affairs, independent of and contrary to that maintained by Gov. Winthrop and the magistracy of Boston at the time,—(the venerable Peter Hobart, whose descendants now happily live among us, and whose spiritual posterity, at least I hope will last as long as time endures),—led the people of your town in a remonstrance against that which they deemed to be an invasion of a municipal right. For that, he and others were summoned before the magistracy in Boston. The good old pastor and his associates, confident that they had not stepped beyond the proper boundaries of their legal rights, refused to go; and, although a fine was subsequently imposed upon them, the strong and dominant will of the ancient men of Hingham was not broken down. And afterwards, when the old pastor was invited to Boston to officiate at the wedding of a person who had formerly been his parishioner, the Magistracy of Boston forbade him to go, declaring, as their to objection him, "that his spirit had been discovered to be adverse to our ecclesiastical and civil government," and because,(so said Winthrop,) Peter Hobart "WAS A BOLD MAN, AND WOULD SPEAK HIS MIND." (Laughter and cheers.) I believe that the men who *will speak their minds* have not yet died out in Hingham, (applause); and I believe that they will endure to the "last syllable of recorded time."

All that I have, friends, to say to-night, bearing upon the political affairs of 1860, is, that I hope all of you will be, as I know you are, "bold men," and that you "will speak your minds." (Cheers.)

I know not, fellow citizens, as yet, nor do you, who the gentlemen are, to be selected as the standard bearers of the opposing parties to that Republican organization of which I am the unworthy representative. There are three parties to oppose us—three parties, each with creed or purpose separate from, independent of, and opposed to ours, and opposed to each other. In their ranks they number honest, intelligent, patriotic and able men. I doubt not that they too will speak their minds, and that each one, according to the forms of its own organization, and according to the proprieties which, in their best judgment, befit the occasion, will select their candidates. Their candidates, all of them, will be before you. From them all you will select.

I hope I may venture to add a word bearing upon the befitting method for the conduct, not of this campaign only, but of all political campaigns. I speak to my political associates as well as to those who may oppose my party at the polls. My suggestion and advice shall be presented to you in the form of a story. Once, in ancient times, an Arab chieftain owned a beautiful Arabian mare. She was the pet of his household and the joy of his eyes; fleet as the wind, nimble as the breezes, and fair (so said the Arab story,) as the moon. A neighboring chieftain sought to possess the steed, but money would not win from his tent nor from his hand the horse he loved. By and by, full of craft, as well as selfishness, the disappointed chieftain covered himself with rags, bent down as if broken by age and grief, and, crouching by the wayside as the owner of the mare careered along upon his proud and prancing steed, he held out his hand, and, with faint and pitiful accents, besought him, that, for the love of God, he would take up a poor worn and weary and sickened wayfarer, and carry him to some place of shelter. Moved by the sad appeal, he dismounted, and, lifting the pretended beggar, placed him upon the back of his steed. Once mounted, the beggar revealed himself a robber. It was the disappointed neighbor, who by craft and guile, had sought to possess himself of the much coveted steed. Swinging his turban aloft, and putting spurs to the flanks of the mare, he cried aloud, in accents of defiant taunt, "I have won your mare at last,"—and passed away. Soon the owner met the robber, and accosted him. Said he, "I have not told to any mortal ear the story of my loss, I will never pursue you, nor seek to avenge my wrong at the hand of human law. I only ask that you may never tell the tale to any other man. I took you up in what I supposed to be the want and grief and pain of your poor humanity, for the love of God and from a sentiment of human pity. If I or you should tell that tale to human ears, and so unbelievable a thing should get abroad among our countrymen, some poor stricken son of sorrow, who may, in honest grief and poverty, extend his hand for alms, and seek the aid of his fellow, may be suspected of imposture like your own; and I would not that any human sympathy should go unspent, or any human want or sorrow pass unrelieved, by reason of your craft and wickedness weakening the faith of man in his brother." If in any one of those who may be candidates for your political favor, now or hereafter, you shall perceive any evidence of weakness, any error of speech, or doctrine, or life, which to your judgment may seem to be a blunder or a wrong, judge, if you will, but judge, I pray you, as you would preserve the fresh heart of sweet and fair humanity. Help not me by aspersion of any one whose error, if error he has committed, shall have been due to his judgment and not to his heart. There are, in the weary ways of this work-day world, in the bustle and hurry and competitions of a careful and anxious life—there are causes and temptations enough to lead us away from and make us forget what we owe to the heart itself, what we owe to the dear, sweet impulse of a common human love. Judge all men, if you will, by the strictest standard of intellectual fitness, but always pardon every thing to the weakness, if weakness it be, that only loved God's poor too well.

We have, my friends, a grand, a beautiful, and a glorious heritage,—consecrated, by our father's blood and our mother's prayers, by the fidelity and industry and patriotism of their children, to you and to God. "You have a Sparta—ornament it and preserve it." This is your gift—this broad, fair land. These teeming fields, these healthful airs, these skies, which almost "rain down fatness," these institutions, where the freedom of human labor gives to every man an opportunity, to every woman the chance, and to every child the promise of an independent, honest, happy existence. You have here no man with power to hold the mastery over heart, vote, judgment, or voice. It is all yours—all mine. Without it, what were the "promised land" itself? With it, even out of the sands we may suck up riches. Stand by, friends and fellow citizens, according to the measure and method of your faith and conviction, stand by these grand, historic, venerable and consecrated institutions of Massachusetts! Hold all your political parties up to the principles of your fathers, to the institutions which have made you happy, wealthy, independent, and your children free! We have a State, and we have a confederated Union. You and I are loyal to one and the other and to both. We are all here lovers of Union and Liberty. We believe in the just and equal rights of man, as the self-evident truth our fathers wrote it down to be in the immortal Declaration of our National Independence. (Applause.) We all mean, for whatever names we vote, to preserve and to work out to ultimate triumph the doctrines of the Declaration and of the Preamble to the Constitution of our Union. We mean to perpetuate LIBERTY to the latest time and to the last posterity. (Great cheering.) And we mean to do it, through the forms, social and political, through the organizations of society and of the State, which we find extant,—not being radical in the sense of destructiveness, but radical in the honest sense of preserving, conserving and perpetuating the good and the true. (Renewed cheering.) Other men, elsewhere, may prophecy evil; other men may forebode evil days and times and transactions to come, which shall threaten our institutions, which shall threaten to weaken our government, or to weaken our love for it; but we know better. (Enthusiastic applause.) Our hearts are firmly anchored here. We believe in the right, we believe in the competency, and we believe in the success of self-government—a government by the people. We are Democrats of the old school; Democrats in the blood, in the bone, in the heart; by the convictions of our judgment, and by the experience of ourselves and of our fathers, and we are not to be frightened. (Renewed and vociferous cheering.) No matter what shall come to this State and to this Union of States, we all shall stand. When the fire waxes hot, still shall we stand; if the tempest rages, there shall we stand; and where danger is thickest, there shall we be We shall have faith to stand there, like that old soldier of the Revolution, who was posted by Col. Horrey, at an imminent point of danger, who cried out to his commander, "Captain, I am shot." "No matter—stand!" Again he cries out, "Captain, the red-coats have hit me again." "Let them fire—stand!" Once more he cries out, "Oh, captain, they have shot me again." "Stand, brave comrade, and draw their fire!" (Laughter and applause.) The manly hearts, the conservative judgment, the unfailing fidelity, of people such as you—Republicans, Union-men, Democrats of Hingham—against whatever storm, in the midst of whatever peril, in spite of whatever evil forebodings, will save the Union and the State. We shall have here, as we have had in the past, all the conflicts of parties, but we shall perpetuate, as we have done, and our fathers before us in the past, this government, because we believe in the principles upon which it is founded. No mere mechanism, none of the chances of politics, none of the policies of wise men, can save a State, preserve a people, and perpetuate liberty. Only on the intelligent virtue of the masses of men and women, and their intelligent faith in fundamental truth can free institutions stand and endure. I care not if you sweep away Republicanism, (technically so called) from Massachusetts; I will trust it to the Bell men, to the Democrats, according to Douglas, or Breckinridge, that they would nail the flag of Liberty to the mast, and if the old ship went down their forms would sink with it beneath the wave. And in any exigency of the States would trust our adopted citizens of Massachusetts "to take up the parable," and prophecy good of our American Israel.

I tell you, that although I believe in the principles of the Republican party as the only sound political faith of to-day, although I believe that the Republican organization is the only one adapted to meet the exigencies of the time, and although I believe that their organization ought to be perpetuated and that their nominees ought to be elected (loud laughter and cheers),—if I did not think so I would not stand (renewed cheering),—yet I believe in the religious and political education of our people more than I believe in all things else. I believe in the fitness of my fellow-citizens to accept the responsibilities of whatever power it may please Providence to bestow upon them, and that, whosoever may have possession of a majority of votes, in Massachusetts, at least, we shall always find a faithful, loyal, independent and patriotic people.

And now, fellow-citizens, having wearied you, I fear, by this too tedious address, I commend to you, with a repetition of my hearty, heartfelt, humble and sincere gratitude, the consideration of the duties and responsibilities of the hour.

This, fellow-citizens, is no moment of exultation to me. I am not insensible to the allurements of place, to the prize of public honor; but I am far more conscious, and I much more deeply feel the weight of responsibility which popular favor and the possession of place and power imposes upon the citizen who holds them. I cannot find it in my heart to exult, that by the favor of the people of the commonwealth I may sit in the Executive chair of the State, which has been filled and adorned by men of the present and past time, illustrious for their virtues, illustrious for their public services, and brilliant by the possession of genius and noble hearts. I feel that, by unequal steps I shall only follow a great way after them, and shall possibly, with the best purposes, defeat and disappoint the expectations of the warmest and most trusting friends. I hope and pray that nought I fear may come to pass, and that all I hope of capacity and purpose to do you good and to serve the State, whether in public or in private, in my day and generation, may be fulfilled.

And now, fellow-citizens of Hingham, it only remains to me tonight to say once more, that for this friendly and neighborly sympathy and recognition, you have the homage of my grateful thanks. I wish my house was as large as my heart, that you might all come in. I bid you welcome here. Come, those who can; and those who cannot find an entrance now beneath my roof, come another time. Come when you will; I am here, and my latch string is out! (Enthusiastic and prolonged cheering.)

Now, with an affectionate and hearty "Good night," I seek only the gratification of shaking hands with as many of you as I may.

Nine hearty cheers were given for Mr. Andrew, at the conclusion of his speech; the band playing a lively air, and the blaze of numerous rockets adding brilliancy and beauty to the joyous scene.

The procession then re-formed, and again marched through the street, to the enlivening music of the band, cheering enthusiastically at various points, and, later in the evening, returning to Mr. Andrew's house, where refreshments had been bountifully provided, again greeted their friend, and partook of his cheer. The occasion, altogether, was one most gratifying and delightful, and will doubtless be long remembered with pleasure by all who participated in it. The number present when Mr. Andrew spoke must have been somewhere between two and three thousand, who were enthusiastic in their demonstrations of affectionate regard. Well may the Republican candidate be proud of his friends and neighbors; well, too, may they be proud of him.

Serenade to John A. Andrew.

GREAT GATHERING IN CHARLES STREET.

SPEECH OF MR. ANDREW.

Last evening the Republican nominee for Governor was serenaded at the residence of Daniel Davies, Esq., No. 68 Charles street. The street in front of the house was thronged with people at an early hour, and among them were many ladies, who patiently waited until half-past nine o'clock for the arrival of the procession from Bowdoin square. At that hour the Lincoln Guard No. 1 escorted to the place the Rail Splitter's Battalion, together with a large number of people who had assembled at the head-quarters of the battalion. The Chelsea Brass Band headed the procession, and as it marched down Beacon street the lanterns and torches presented a fine appearance.

Upon their arrival the band played "Hail Columbia" and the "Star Spangled Banner," and after nine enthusiastic cheers for Mr. Andrew, that gentleman appeared at the window, accompanied by Charles B Hall, Esq., who introduced him briefly, claiming that Mr. Andrew was entitled to the office of Governor, for his dignified and honorable bearing upon all occasions, public and private—for his integrity and honesty of purpose, his unquestioned ability, and unblemished moral character. Whenever, said Mr. Hall, such claims are presented to the citizens of this Commonwealth, they must and will be responded to by tens of thousands majority over all opposition.

Mr. Andrew then stepped upon the platform, and was received with the firing of rockets, music by the band, and loud cheers from the assembled thousands. Silence being restored, he delivered the following speech. We quote from the verbatim report in the

Advertiser, which has since been carefully corrected for insertion in the *Traveller:—*

Mr. Andrew's Speech.

Fellow-Citizens and Brother Republicans of Boston:

The grand enthusiastic welcome with which this vast and uncounted concourse of my fellow-citizens have been pleased to greet my humble presence here to-night, fills me with emotions strange and engrossing, struggling with each other for utterance and expression, which your imaginations may conceive, but which no poor words or voice of mine can utter. I can only, gentlemen Republicans of Boston, in feeble accents and with palpitating heart, in simple phrase say, I thank you. (Cheers.) My heart and voice consent together while they cry out, I thank you, friends and brother republicans. (Enthusiastic cheering.) Not unto me, not unto me is this ovation given; but to that grand Republican cause, that great and conquering cause of THE PEOPLE, inaugurated for the year 1860 at the Chicago Convention, which is now advancing, with victorious hosts, to the conquests of liberty (Applause.) Out of the Egypt of a long bondage are you now emerging, ("good") and not now, as you have been, in years before, with faint and feeble accents struggling to speak the trumpet note of victory. It leaps with one consent from the unanimous lips of a vast majority of the American people. (Great applause.) By the faith of *Abraham*, (prolonged and hearty applause and three cheers for Lincoln,) and with the courage of Hannibal, (renewed cheering) Republicanism is bound to conquer.

You have established a communication of mind and heart, running from the sounding shores of Maine, across the Alleghanies, over the broad and rolling prairies of the West, climbing the Rocky Mountains, and reaching at last those outposts of civilization upon the shores of the Pacific sea. (A voice, "Glory to Vermont.") Maine and Oregon, the easternmost and westernmost States of this grand confederacy of the free, will be found enrolling their electoral votes for Lincoln and Hamlin. (Cheers). Vermont has spoken already. (Cheers and cries of "good.") The home of Edward Bates and Frank Blair, by the voice of the freemen of St. Louis, in a slaveholding Commonwealth, has began to exhibit the evidence that Missouri ere long will be found enrolled among the posts of freedom. No longer can the Republican party be assailed by the taunts of opponents charging its organization, its men, its principles and its future destiny, with any of the aspersions that linger around the name of "sectionalism." In Maryland, in Virginia, in Kentucky, in Missouri—the homes of the Blairs, elder and younger, of Bates, and of Cassius M. Clay —you have your representatives and your men. (Applause). This, fellow-citizens, is the inauguration of your movement, which will go on with increasing zeal and with increasing courage of heart and energy of purpose, until you shall see yourselves in possession of the high places of power.

I speak to you, gentlemen, as a popular representation of the people—as an organized, or, if you please, an unorganized body, but still a popular representation of the people. You will permit me, perhaps—regarding you for the moment in that capacity—to say a single word to you. I have ventured to call this the cause of the people. Sometimes men call it the cause of a section; sometimes the cause of a race: I regard it as the cause of ALL. (Cheering and cries of "Good.") We have in the nation to-day three or four parties—I hardly know which—contending for the support and votes of the people; the party led by Lincoln and Hamlin—the Republican organization; the democratic party—sectional certainly, divided now into two sections—(loud laughing and applause)—one of them affirmatively and declaratively in favor of slavery, and the other as distinctively opposed to freedom. (Laughter.) And yet, such is the loving fraternity existing between the two, that I have seen from the Richmond Enquirer, the representative press of Breckinridge in Virginia, a threat to hang Judge Douglas of Illinois, who is the representative man of the other organization. (Laughter and a shout of "he ought to be hung.") You have also the party of Bell and Everett, called by the name of the "Constitutional Union party;" the "Constitutional Union party," standing on a platform, it is said, which no man has ever read or even seen. (Laughter.) It declares itself to be no geographical party—knowing no North, no South, no East, no West, no anywhere, and *no nothing*. (Laughter and cheers.) It propounds for its creed "the Union, Constitution, and the enforcement of the laws"—(a voice, "Slave laws")—as if nobody before, since America was discovered, had ascertained that there is a Constitution, that there is a Union, and that we express ourselves by written laws. But what interpretation of the Constitution, and what theory for the preservation of the Union and the perpetuation of liberty, what interpretation of the laws or what system of laws they desire, they do not give us to understand, nor even to guess.

I had supposed, fellow-citizens, that this was a government of the people, and I take exception to the very phraseology of the final clause of that which they call their platform, (which platform is none) "the enforcement of the laws."

What a creed is that, fellow-citizens, for a democratic-republican government or party! The "*enforcement* of the laws!" Who, I pray you, fellow-citizens, enforces the laws? Who are to enforce the laws in a government like ours? Who but the people? (A voice, "that's so.") The people both make the laws, and obey them when they are made. (A voice, "amen.") With us the enforcement of the laws, gentlemen, is the act of the people upon the few exceptional persons who refuse obedience. The vast, the conquering and overwhelming majority of the people, whose country's laws are written in their hearts, enforce the laws (applause and cries of "good") against the disobedient, the vicious and wicked who would trample upon the laws and set them at naught, and attack the security, peace and welfare of the whole.

Such "enforcement," if they will insist on the word, is done always, and naturally as water runs down hill. I say, fellow-citizens, that in a country like ours, he has no conception of the just uses of government, of the significance of a party creed, of the idea, the central idea of our institutions, who proclaims any other theory in regard to the relation of the people to the laws, than this. I hold, speaking now as the humble representative of the Republicans of Massachusetts, that *obedience* to the laws is one of the watchwords of a true democracy. Not "enforcement" but *obedience* to the laws. (Applause and shouts of "good.") They thought, I believe, fellow-citizens, they were speaking for some despotic, some crowned or some tyrannical head, wielding a power unconsented to by the people, dictating laws not made by their will, not justified by their relations to the State, not called for by their wants, nor abiding in their hearts. I suspect a mischief lurking beneath that phrase. The people never need be taught to enforce their own laws; and a free people will resent the claim of any enforcement *against* themselves. This people are not slaves; they are free.

What, gentlemen, does that party mean by "the Constitution and the Union"? Who does not believe in a constitution of government—in *the* Constitution, —who, whether of Republican or Democratic relations? I know of none. Who does not believe in a union of these States, and in perpetuating *the* union of these States, in whatever party organization? Here, I know of none. Elsewhere, in other States, there are men holding high public office given them by the people; men holding representative places in the National Congress, who have prophesied evil concerning this Constitution and this Union of ours; but I do not understand that any of these gentlemen of the Bell and Everett organization have singled out those persons—that they have pointed any finger at *them*—that they have administered any rebuke, either in public or private, to *them*. I understand that at this very moment, this party of "the Constitution and the Union" are endeavoring to effect a coalition or fusion between themselves and the Douglas democrats, in the vain hope of carrying the State of New York; and they are also seeking to effect a fusion between themselves and the Breckinridge democrats in New Jersey, with a similar hope of carrying that State against the republicans; and they are seeking everywhere, where they can find ears to listen to their "tinkling brass and empty sound," to manufacture fusions between themselves and all other parties who will but give them their hand upon a common purpose of defeating Lincoln and Hamlin. What a commentary is this upon their fidelity to the Union! If there are any traitors to the Constitution, these men and that party are their accomplices.

Gentlemen, if it were true that while their Convention sat at Baltimore any such danger to the Union existed as that which they claimed to have discovered; as that which the Boston Courier, I understand, constantly shouts or growls—if, I say, there was any such danger existing, I beg to know where that danger is, unless it is to be found in the ranks of their own associates or affiliated parties? Nobody charges upon Republicanism, or upon its adherents, the presence of one disunionist or one disloyal citizen within their ranks. (Loud applause.) Then I humbly ask, upon what principle or theory of fidelity to the Union are they going about the country, endeavoring to make such bargains, compromises, fusions and coalitions. (Cheers.)

Gentlemen, reflect a moment on this tribe of the Bell, the followers of this *peripatetic tintinnabulum*, going about the streets day after day, tinkling them together, not calling them by harmonious strains, of peaceful or of martial music; not even calling them by the fixed conservative "bell in the beltry," but by a travelling representative of uncertain sounds—(laughter)—this "floating bell," making its *false alarms* under our windows! Sirs, it is no compliment to the honesty or intelligence of the American people, to evade the enunciation of distinct opinions. No platform, or creed, or doctrine, is presented by that great Bell-Everett organization today. The Bell men of the South (some of them) declare that as the price of the existence of this government human slavery shall go into all the Territories, and that the establishment of human slavery in the Territories shall be but the premonition of the re-opening of the African slave trade; and that they are entitled to the privilege of buying their negroes, their human flesh, in the cheapest markets. Judge Douglas declares that he does not care whether the extension of slavery is voted up or voted down; and the Bell-Everett party declare that they know nothing whatsoever and think nothing whatsoever upon the subject. But still the controversy goes on. Still the war is raging in the free States and in the slave States. The combat thickens. It exists even between the contending wings of the once united "national democracy," and it finds an expression somewhere in every State Yet the Bell-Everett party has not a word to say. Now, friends and citizens, whosoever takes possession of this government, whichever party holds for the time being, the reins of power, will be obliged to act upon that question, either in one way or the other. Mr. Bell or Mr. Everett, if either of them should become the accidental President of the United States hereafter, must be as "sectional" as Breckinridge on the one hand, or else as "sectional" as Lincoln on the other. There is no middle ground between the two. Judge Douglas professses to discover a middle ground by saying that he "does not care:" but when he reaches the Presidency, if ever he should arrive there, he will be compelled to care, because he will find himself face to face with practical duty. Mr. Bell, should he become the President, cannot ignore the subject, because he too will find himself face to face with a practical duty. Now, I hold it to be an aspersion upon the honesty and intelligence of the people, and upon the popular capacity to comprehend public questions, when party leaders affect to teach that the public mind should neither care for their adjustment, nor take cognizance of their existence. This great question between republicanism and all its adversaries will continue pending until it is intelligently settled. The question has *got to be* settled; it *will be* settled; it *will be* debated. It is of no use to pretend that by mere quiet on the part of a particular Presidential candidate during the campaign, the debate may be shut off. Who is to suppress Gov. Smith of Virginia ("Extra Billy,") with his 2 days' speeches, his files of old newspapers, and his antique almanacs? Who will shut off Judge Douglas, attending but a fortnight during a whole session of Congress, and speaking fifty columns in debate on this very question and not three columns upon all others? Who will suppress Jefferson Davis's resolutions, or Mr. Chesnut's ebullitions? Who will prevent Mr. Crittenden from voting for just such resolutions as Jefferson Davis chooses to present, affirming the most ultra Calhoun doctrines of disunionism? Why, it is patent absurdity upon its face to pretend that by any policy either of audacity, indifference or ignorance, you can establish a peace. You will have to meet this question sometime. It is before you now. It will be discussed in the next Congress and in the Congress after. It will look you in the eye in every debating society, upon every hustings, and in every legislature, until it is ultimately and justly disposed of. The Republican party are determined that it shall be disposed of according to the just rights of the people, and the requirements of a common humanity. (Loud cheers.)

Will you tell me that this is simply a "negro question," and that the Supreme Court of the United States have argued the negro out of the Constitution; that they have drawn an inference and dragged the colored man with the inference after him, out of that immortal document. I tell you, gentlemen, that the power of the Supreme Court to argue the colored man out of the Constitution, may argue you out of it, and me out of it, may argue all of us out of it tomorrow or the day after it. Our fathers declared that Constitution ordained to "secure liberty to ourselves and our posterity." That is the phrase. I would be glad to know how many of you here tonight can trace your lineage back directly to the framers of the Constitution. If the colored man cannot trace his lineage to the framers or adopters of that instrument, can you trace yours back there? Where are you, adopted fellow-citizens—the Frenchmen, the Germans, the Irishmen, who in their own persons, or in the persons of their fathers came over the briny sea, and faced its dangers and its storms, to escape from bondage in other climes and other countries, in order to share the liberties of ours? By what means will they establish their right to a place on the inside of the Constitution, against a Supreme Court who may have any motive to *infer* them out of it? O, sirs, the moment you yield to any such pretence of power, to any such claim or privilege or prerogative as that, you know not whose liberty may be endangered, whose rights may be subverted. I deny, fellow-citizens, upon my responsibility as a man, upon my responsibility as a candidate of the Republicans of Massachusetts—I deny to the Supreme Court of the United States—I deny to any power in this government, legislative, executive or judicial—the right to argue and infer anybody out of the Constitution. (Tremendous applause, and cries of "Good." "We, *the people*," it begins—and the people know who they are themselves, and want no Supreme Court to tell them. (Applause.) We, the people, establish legislatures, choose congressmen, create courts, establish their tenure, vote them their salaries, and grant them their power; and we deny to any of them the right to tell us who we are. (Loud cheers.) No, sirs, the Constitution of the United States is no hidden thing. Its "Scripture" is of no private interpretation. It was made by the people for the people, and adopted by themselves, and upon it they established their government. Will anybody dare to say that the people do not and cannot comprehend the instrument? I tell you sirs, it is the only thing you are *bound* to comprehend this side of the Ten Commandments. They who created it understood it, and they must be assumed by all public officers representing them to have understood it in the sense in which it was written—in the sense in which it was written and interpreted by the unsophisticated minds, by the men of ordinary sense and common understanding by whom it was adopted. And when those men proclaimed, "We, the people," they meant *the people;* using the phrase in its natural and popular sense. The men who fought for liberty and established it, the men who surrounded the Father of his Country, as he led their victorious banner through the fire and blood of a seven years' war, they regarded it alike with John Adams, Benjamin Franklin and Thomas Jefferson; understanding it in the simplest sense of that plain, old, magnificent Anglo-Saxon style in which it was written. No, sirs, from that decision I appeal; from that decision the people have appealed; and a slaveholder of the South, told me, not many months ago, "I appealed, myself, and said to Chief Justice Taney that I had entered the appeal before my colored coachman, for he at least had sense enough to know that he was a man."

But this Republican organization, fellow-citizens, is a party having for its first duty the confirmation of the common popular right in the Territories of the country, within all our national domain, coming under the exclusive jurisdiction of this Federal Government. Squatter Sovereignty, Judge Douglas has told us, will establish liberty; and yet Judge Douglas has told the South in a recent Senatorial speech that this Squatter Sovereignty in New Mexico has carried slavery a degree and a half further North than it ever went before, or ever had the power to go.

You tried the experiment in Texas. I speak now to free white laborers in Boston who may do me the honor to listen to my words to-night. You found Texas a free territory pertaining to the jurisdiction of Mexico. No slavery was permitted there; it was prohibited by the mother country. By American arms, by American prowess and ingenuity, Texas was wrested from Mexico. Your countrymen repealed the ordinance of liberty there as Judge Douglas and his friends repealed the Missouri restriction of 1820.

You attained a broad fair land, larger than France, more fertile and more beautiful than she. Your squatters, the sovereign people resident there, had the power, or exercised the privilege, of writing whatever they pleased upon the blank paper which contained its constitution and code of laws, and they wrote slavery thereon. Did popular sovereignty avail to exclude human servitude from Texas? Texas is a slaveholding State to-day, and has been from the start. Has popular sovereignty succeeded in preserving the liberties of white men? Look at the laws of Texas as they stand now upon the statute book. It is a small State in population, but a great imperial commonwealth in point of territory; and yet thus early in the history of its law, it is written that no white man shall call in question, in the presence or hearing of any other person (although he be white), the lawfulness of the existence of human bondage, under pain of three years imprisonment in the penitentiary. (Cries of "shame.") Such is the description of liberty for free white men that has been secured by the application of Judge Douglas's principle in Texas! Go to every other slaveholding State, and the same description of laws prevails. Wherever slavery gains a foothold in any territory, there the men who own the slave own also the land. By owning the slaves they crowd out and drive away, discourage and put down, all experiments at successful free white labor. Owning the labor and owing the land, they subsidize the press, they silence the pulpit, they control the hustings and they make the laws; taking care to apportion the taxes so as to protect slavery and discourage freedom. You will find, gentlemen, if you go there with your sons, in the hope of establishing homes for yourself and them—you will find alongside of you a wealthy and respectable gentleman from Tennessee or South Carolina, who has established himself there with five hundred African slaves. He has bought up a thousand acres of soil, and established a system of espionage upon the other settlers. All your conduct, every hour of your day, every moment of your night, every accent of your voice, every word you speak, every song you sing, every prayer you utter to Heaven, is under that constant system of espionage. You recede, free white labor recedes, free white men recede, and all the institutions of freedom recede before him and his slavery, as health recedes before the pestilence. Try it! A slaveholder from Maryland told me but a few weeks ago that he could look out of the windows of his house, and for miles around him see no land that was not owned by aristocratic landholders, by men of wealth. "Upon my own plantation," said he, "I have hutted divers free white American-born families, too poor to obtain the means of living or buying a residence of their own, and who would not be permitted to become purchasers of land. In all that pertains to the comforts and decencies of life, they are far below the colored slaves whom I myself own" That is the story of a slaveholder in Maryland, and Maryland is a northern slaveholding State upon the borders of free commonwealths, and a commonwealth to which our friend Mr. Thayer of Worcester, in a recent address to his constituents, pointed as one which illustrates the power of free labor to drive out slavery. I know, fellow citizens, that one day slavery will be excluded from Maryland, no matter what system of laws may prevail; because I know that the providence of God is stronger than the counsels of men. It will die out there, because it will ultimately vanish from the face of the earth. It will be exterminated there, because the day shall surely dawn when the whole family of man shall become one upon a sanctified earth, as it assuredly shall be in a glorified Heaven. (Enthusiastic applause) But I do not mean to wait. I, as one humble citizen of Massachusetts, do not intend to wait for the providence of God by miracle or otherwise to perform the work assigned to human instrumentality. I confess I have no political power to act directly or indirectly upon any institution or practice peculiar to any other Commonwealth than Massachusetts But I have a constitutional political power to speak, to vote and to act touching the establishment and perpetuation of any institution of which the government can take cognizance within any territory over which the American flag floats, and where the national government has jurisdiction exclusively to itself. (Four cheers and "that's the talk.") Up to the full extent of whatever political power, as a man, as a citizen, or as a magistrate I may possess, I mean to go. (Hearty applause and cries of "good.") Just up to that and no further. I sympathize with Hungary, bound down and trodden beneath the hoofs of the war-horses of Austria. My heart bleeds for poor oppressed and suffering Italy to-night. Every throb and pulsation of this beating frame leaps out in joyous and exhilarating emotion as I hear of the stormy conquests of Garibaldi. (Great enthusiasm) I hope to see the day when the people of France, no longer sitting down in stolid content beneath the orderly despotism of a second Napoleon, may rise in the might of regenerated and intelligent freemen, and establish a liberty as grand, as certain, as brilliant and as lasting as any that ever set upon the peak of the heaven crowned Alps. (Prolonged and hearty cheering.) But I do not mean, I do not propose that the legislature of Massachusetts, or the Congress of the United States should vote liberty to Hungary, to France, or to Italy. I know that we have no power politically, by voice or vote to lift from Ireland any institutions or practices of the British Parliament which oppress that long suffering people. I am well aware that the legislature of Massachusetts, that the Congress of the United States, have as little power as the Hull town-meeting to abolish slavery in Virginia and Carolina; and I would as soon think of proposing such a vote before that respectable body of my fellow-citizens—almost every one of whom I know—in the town hall, as I would before the grand representative assembly of the whole American Confederacy, and I should as soon think of being afraid that Hull would abolish slavery in Lousiana, as that the American Congress would abolish it by a vote in South Carolina.

Sirs, this old appeal to your fears is just about worn out. I have always noticed that the first step toward making a man a rascal is to make him a coward. (Loud applause.) The practical application which I beg leave to make of that remark, is, that in 1856, although every doctrine and principle peculiar to the Republican organization of that year and of the present, was substantially admitted by the Whig State Committee of Massachusetts, yet those gentlemen, practising under their fears, misled by the forebodings they professed, and I hope honestly entertained, allowed themselves to be diverted from the support of the gallant Fremont, allowed themselves to use their influence and their purses for the purpose of establishing a similar organization in aid of Mr. Fillmore in the State of Pennsylvania, and by that means co-operated in the rendition of the vote of Pennsylvania and Indiana for James Buchanan, whose little finger in the cause and in all the abominable work of despotism has, during his four years, been thicker than the loins of Franklin Pierce, (Laughter and cheers.) And now, to-night, those very gentleman, that very class of Optimists and Quietists—gentlemen of the very highest social position, of the utmost purity of private life, of great and brilliant powers and acquisitions of intellect,—are laying the foundation for the accomplishment (if it is possible) of the same defeat of liberty now. It remains to be seen whether that which has been practised once with such success can be accomplished again. (A voice, "It can't be done.") I think it cannot be done. (Applause.) No sirs, it *cannot* be done. Indiana, which gave her vote for James Buchanan in 1856, is alive. From the northern boundary to the Ohio river the watch-fires of liberty burn on every hill, and they shine over every valley. Indianapolis has just seen the largest gathering of the people of Indiana that ever came together for any purpose either political or otherwise, in any of the vast commonwealths of the West. That State, upon my conscience, I believe to be secure. (Great cheering.) The representatives of Pennsylvania in the Chicago Convention declared to us of New England that with Abraham Lincoln as the standard-bearer of the republican party, Pennsylvania was secure. Events are fulfilling the promise. (Applause.) It remains only for you to say whether the support of Massachusetts and of every intelligent freeman of Massachusetts shall be given to this cause—this cause, which is for the establishment of liberty, the perpetuation of the Union, and the immortality of the Constitution. They will assail us on every side; they will meet us at every turn. But who cares for taunt or jibe, or sneer, who knows that he is right; who fears the assaults of friend or foe, the malignity of party presses, the trembling of weak-kneed friends, the incertitude of those who are always hesitating, the charge and counter-charge of adversaries, the war of elements and the shock of worlds, if he knows he is right? (Cheers)

Gentlemen, it was not my purpose to detain you thus long when you did me the honor to make this evening call. (Loud shouts of "go on,") I wish, fellow-citizens, it was in my power to address you upon several topics connected with the campaign, under circumstances as safe and convenient for you to stand and listen. Perhaps at some future time it may be. (Applause and cries of "good.") If the occasion arises, Heaven helping me, I shall be there. (Renewed cheers.) No matter what exigencies this campaign may disclose, whatever may be its perils, I shall meet them, shielded by the protection of your sympathies and trusting that the God of liberty will maintain his cause. Whatever may come, my voice is clear, my heart is strong, my purpose is fixed and my confidence assured.

"Now welcome be Cumberland's steed to the shock!"

At the close of Mr. Andrew's address, he was greeted with vociferous applause.

The procession then returned home, through Mount Vernon, Hancock and Cambridge streets, to Bowdoin Square. As they passed the residence of Hon. Charles Sumner, on Hancock street, loud and hearty cheers were given for him. The Lincoln Guard, after an interchange of cheering with the Rail Splitters' Battalion in front of their headquarters, marched through Court and Washington streets, to their headquarters, accompanied by the Band.

SPEECH

OF

JOHN A. ANDREW, ESQ.,

At the Meeting held in the Tremont Temple, Nov. 18, 1859, for the Relief of the Family of John Brown.

At the conclusion of Rev. Dr. Neale's prayer, Mr. Andrew said:—

Ladies and Gentlemen,—Obedient to the commands of the gentlemen who arranged the meeting on this occasion, I am here present to occupy the simple and inarduous duties of chairman. They do not impose upon me the office of speech, and I hardly deem it consistent with the proprieties of the position I hold. It simply is incumbent upon me to say a simple word by way of explanation, of the order and arrangement and principles of this meeting, and to present to you the distinguished and eloquent friends who have complied with the invitation of the committee, and are here present to address this audience. Many hearts were touched by the words of John Brown, in a recent letter to Lydia Maria Child:—

"I have at home a wife and three young daughters, the youngest but little over five years old, the oldest nearly sixteen. I also have two daughters-in-law, whose husbands have both fallen near me here. There is also another widow, Mrs. Thompson, whose husband fell here. Whether she is a mother or not, I cannot say. I have a middle-aged son, who has been, in some degree, a cripple from his childhood, who would have as much as he could well do to earn a living. He has not enough to clothe himself for the winter comfortably."

John Brown and his companions in the conflict at Harper's Ferry, those who fell there and those who are to suffer upon the scaffold, are victims or martyrs to an idea. There is an irresistible conflict (great applause) between freedom and slavery, as old and as immortal as the irrepressible conflict between right and wrong. They are among the martyrs of that conflict.

I pause not now to consider, because it is wholly outside of the duty or the thought of this assembly to-night, whether the enterprise of John Brown and his associates in Virginia was wise or foolish, right or wrong; I only know that whether the enterprise itself was one or the other, John Brown himself is right (Applause.) I sympathize with the man. I sympathize with the idea because I sympathize with and believe in the eternal right. They who are dependent upon him, and his sons and his associates in the battle at Harper's Ferry, have a right to call upon us who have professed to believe, or who have in any manner or measure taught, the doctrine of the rights of man as applied to the colored slaves of the South, to stand by them in their bereavement, whether those husbands and fathers and brothers were right or wrong. (Applause.) And therefore we have met to take counsel together, and assist each other in the arrangement and apportionment of means for the purpose of securing to those widowed and bereaved wives and families the necessities of mere mortal existence, which the striking down of husbands and sons and brothers has left them bereft of. The committee for this evening had invited to address you the Rev. Mr. Manning, Mr. Ralph Waldo Emerson, and Mr. Wendell Phillips. Added to these gentlemen was the Rev. George H. Hepworth. Mr. Manning, Mr. Emerson and Mr. Phillips are here to speak for themselves.

[Mr. Andrew here read a letter from Rev. Mr. Hepworth, excusing himself from attending the meeting, and then proceeded:—]

It was not suspected by anybody that there were two sides to the question whether John Brown's wife and children should be left to starve or not. (Long continued applause.) On that issue I expect no considerable acrimony of debate between the gentlemen of extreme orthodoxy and of extreme heterodoxy whom I shall have the honor hereafter to present to you upon this platform. Gentlemen, all of them, of marked, of intelligent, of decided opinions, and of entire respect for themselves and for their own individuality, they will each present such aspect of this great cause, and of this most touching and pathetic case, as occurs to them. It will not compromise Mr. Phillips that he sits upon a platform consecrated by the prayer of the Rev. Dr. Neale, and it will not compromise the Rev. Mr. Manning that he works tonight side by side and hand in hand with Ralph Waldo Emerson, in the cause of God and humanity. (Applause.) Standing in the valley of the shadow of death,—looking, each man, from himself towards that infinite and eternal centre of life and love and power, the Infinite Father,—all difference between us mortals and men becomes dwarfed into infinite littleness. We are tonight in the presence of a great and awful sorrow, which has fallen like a pall upon many families, whose hearts fail, whose affections are lacerated, and whose hopes are crushed—all of hope left upon earth destroyed by an event which, under the Providence of God, I pray may be overruled for that good which was contemplated and intended by John Brown himself. But this is not my occasion for words. I have only to invite you, friends, to listen with affectionate interest and feeling hearts to what you shall hear from hence tonight, and by practical sympathy and material help, assuage those sufferings and those griefs.

Mr. Andrew then described the means by which it was proposed to raise money for the aid of Brown's family, and concluded by introducing the Rev. Mr. Manning, pastor of the Old South Church.

HARPER'S FERRY INVESTIGATING COMMITTEE.

TESTIMONY OF JOHN A. ANDREW.

As a matter of interest to the people of Massachusetts at the present time, we present for their careful perusal the testimony of John A. Andrew, the Republican candidate for Governor, before the Harper's Ferry Investigating Committee of the Senate, on the 9th of February, 1860:

It is taken from the official report of the proceedings of the Committee published by order of the Senate, and is therefore of undoubted accuracy.

FEBRUARY 9, 1860.

JOHN A. ANDREW sworn and examined.

By the Chairman:

Question. Will you please to state where you reside, and what your occupation is?

Answer. My home is Boston, Massachusetts, and I am a practitioner of law in Boston.

Question. Will you state whether you engaged counsel to defend John Brown, who was recently executed in Virginia for offences against the laws of that State, on his indictment and trial?

Answer. I engaged the Hon. Samuel Chilton of Washington, who assisted in the defence of Captain John Brown, at Charlestown, and also the Hon. William Green of Richmond, Virginia, who assisted Mr. Chilton in relation to the prosecution of a writ of error. The fact of the action of these gentlemen is not personally known to me of my own knowledge; I only know it by correspondence and public report. I never had the pleasure of being in Virginia.

Question. Will you please to state under what circumstances you engaged them as counsel; what led you to do it; what was the reason why you engaged them?

The Witness. The operative motive on my mind?

The Chairman. Any reasons connected with it —who employed or engaged you, or why you did it.

Answer. If my motives are deemed——

The Chairman. Not your motives at all. What I want to know is, at whose instance were counsel employed in Virginia, and who furnished the compensation to the counsel?

The Witness. As I was about to remark, if it is desired by the committee to know what operated on my mind, and led to the employment of these gentlemen through my intervention, I will state with entire freedom, and I hope the gentlemen of the committee will not regard anything I may say as intended to be at all disrespectful to them or to Virginia. When the intelligence reached Boston by telegraph that the local court in Jefferson county, Virginia, was proceeding to the trial of John Brown and one of his associates, with such speed and hurried action on its part as to render it probable that there was to be no sufficient opportunity to make a full and complete defence, and under such circumstances as that the physical condition of the men themselves seemed to render it entirely improbable that they could prepare a defence with propriety, it struck my mind, and the minds of various other gentlemen whom I met with in the ordinary avocations of my business, in the street, the office, the court rooms, and otherwise, as being a judicial outrage. I certainly felt it to be such. It was wholly unlike anything I had ever known or heard of in my practice as a lawyer. When some persons had been indicted for kidnapping in Massachusetts last September, the court gave General Cushing, their counsel, two or three months after their arraignment before he was required even to file a plea. Various gentlemen said to me, without respect of party or person, "You, Mr. Andrew, are known to be a lawyer of anti-slavery sentiments, or of Republican sentiments, and of considerable readiness to act on any occasion which seems to you to be proper; why do not you go to Virginia and volunteer to defend Captain Brown?" Without remembering the names of persons who spoke to me, I should not think it strange if twenty men, of all shades of opinion, might have made that remark; and many persons thought that the circumstances under which this proceeding was going on in Virginia were such as to tend to increase rather than to diminish the ill feeling that the unfortunate foray of Captain Brown had already excited. I said to others, and said to myself, "If I should go to Virginia, I, a Republican lawyer and a Massachusetts man, should be before a court and jury so little in sympathy with myself that I should be quite as much on trial as my client would be. Besides that, I am a stranger to the local jurisprudence and practice of Virginia," (although I was somewhat familiar with the reports, and not unfamiliar with some books, particularly I remember Mr. Robinson's practice, which I read with a great deal of pleasure.) Knowing nobody sufficiently well to take that liberty with him, save Judge Montgomery Blair, of Washington, I at once wrote to him a letter, of which I think I kept no copy—I feel very sure I did not—stating to him how I felt about it and how other gentlemen felt, and I think I also suggested that I thought if Captain Brown was in Massachusetts, charged with any crime, he would not only have a long time given to him to enable his friends to examine into the state of his mind, with a view to testing its sanity, but that it did seem to me an investigation would result in finding testimony, all the way from Boston to Kansas, which would tend to prove him insane. That suggestion I made in the letter, and I made it merely as the result of an inference, not as the result of any facts of which I had personal knowledge. I also said that if Judge Blair would himself go to Virginia, undertake the cause, and see that Captain Brown had a complete and appropriate defense, according to the laws of the jurisdiction where he was indicted, raising whatever questions of law ought to be raised, and having them heard before the tribunal of ultimate resort, I would guaranty to him a proper and honorable compensation; or if he was not of opinion that he ought to go, or if he could not go in person, I would adopt his selection of any other gentleman of the bar, and would guaranty his compensation; that I desired a gentleman familiar with the institutions, practice, and jurisprudence of Virginia, and whose personal presence would not prejudice his client; the result was the employment of Mr. Chilton. After Mr. Chilton had retired from Charlestown, either in consequence of a letter written by himself to me, or a letter written on his behalf by somebody else, I was led to offer, in the same feeling and with the same general view and purpose, a fee of $300 (fixing it in my own mind, because there was but little time to make any bargain about it) to any gentlemen from Richmond whom Mr. Chilton should himself select as an associate. Mr. Daniel of Richmond and Mr. Green were both spoken of. Mr. Daniel declined, on account of his other engagements, and his letter was sent to me. He recommended Mr. Green. Mr. Green was retained, and I honored the drafts to the amount of Mr. Chilton's fee of $1000, and Mr. Green's fee of $300. In undertaking to retain and pay these gentlemen, I acted self-moved, except in so far as my own opinion and judgment was influenced by the general remarks of which I have spoken, made to me by friends and neighbors and fellow-citizens of Boston, of various descriptions and opinions. In my letter to Judge

Blair, I said I make this application to you in behalf of the friends or of friends of Captain Brown. I felt justified in using that expression; because I could safely call all of us who desired a fair trial of a man—of whom we had, for a long time, entertained a good opinion as an honest man—his *friends.* I felt, also, that I could fairly say, if it were needful, that the application was made in behalf of his family, because I was sure that I must be serving the welfare of a man's family, in seeking to secure for him a good defence. I wished, also, so to express myself as not to place Mr. Blair, nor any other counsel whom he might employ in his stead, in any relation of delicacy towards myself, of the same profession. If I had offered the money as out of my own pocket, or upon my own risk, my friend, Mr. Blair, or any other lawyer, would have doubtless felt a certain delicacy in accepting the retainer, coming from a brother lawyer, influenced only by public or benevolent considerations. I adopted phraseology, therefore, which would steer clear of that delicacy of relation which a direct statement of my precise position would have involved.

Question. Will you state how this money was furnished, and by whom furnished? If you can, give the names.

Answer. Without regard to my being in full possession or not, I accepted the drafts as they were drawn on me, and the money was furnished by A., B., & C., whom I might happen to meet in business, or in pleasure, or at church.

Question. Was the money furnished at your request, or was it voluntarily proffered?

Answer. I stated to various gentlemen—gentlemen whom I might meet at dinner; gentlemen whom I met at church, in the court house; and any others whom I might perhaps take pains to fall in with—what I had done, making the remark, "If you approve of my conduct and think it is right, please to give anything towards the fund which you feel free to give."

Various gentlemen, friends of mine, I remember, came in and offered me money which they had collected on the street, as they told me, on State street, on 'Change, anywhere, having said to people: "Mr. Andrew has assumed responsibility for the defence of John Brown, stating the circumstances; do you desire to give anything towards relieving him from the pecuniary responsibility he has undertaken?" In that way the money came in. Some gentlemen, perhaps, would give five dollars, and some fifty dollars. I knew some of the donors; others I did not know. For example, I remember that I asked a gentleman to state the fact of what I had done, as he might have opportunity, among the members of the Legislature, the General Court of Massachusetts, then in session, and almost everybody in the Legislature knew me personally or knew something about me. The result was that some of the money came from them. It came from merchants, and lawyers, and legislators, and perhaps ladies, although I do not know that any ladies gave anything towards it of my own knowledge.

Question. Will you state, sir, whether your reason for volunteering your aid in this matter, and the representations that you made to others, or what induced you to act as you state you did act, was founded on the impression that Brown was not going to have a fair or just trial, or was it founded on a disposition to aid in his defence, because of his career against the institution of slavery?

Answer. Well, sir, I know—

Question. In other words, if you had no impressions that the trial was not one fairly and properly conducted, would you have acted as you did, in getting money for his defence, only from a desire to serve him because of the career in which he was embarked?

Answer. I am quite clear on that point, putting the question in that way. As you, sir, first proposed the question, it was a little complex and intricate. Had I felt that Captain Brown and his associates were in the way to a full and complete opportunity for a fair judicial investigation into all their rights according to the laws of the jurisdiction within which they were, I have no reason to suppose that I should have interfered. I should have felt that I had no occasion to interfere. I had known about old Mr. Brown for several years and I approved a great deal which I had heard of touching his career in Kansas; I thought he had been an honest, and conscientious, and useful assistant of the Free State cause. My impression of him was derived from many sources. I had never seen him but once in my life, and then only for a few moments. I say in frankness that I felt a certain sympathy for a man who had, as I thought, been useful in behalf of a great cause in which I was interested. I had no sympathy with his peculiar conduct touching which he was then indicted. I felt injured by that, personally, as a Republican.

Question. Suppose the only difficulty connected with his trial as you heard, had been the want of means, would you and your friends then have volunteered to furnish the means to employ counsel?

Answer. It is not easy, Mr. Chairman, for one man to speak as to another's motives. I can only speak as to my own; and you have now put a question which embarrasses me to this extent: It is unpleasant for a man to blow the trumpet of his own virtue, and I am sorry to be asked to state to what extent I may be a benevolent man, or otherwise. I can only give you one little circumstance, as an illustration of what I might do under such circumstances. Last year a man was convicted in Boston for piracy, and sentenced to be hanged. I had never seen him, to speak to him, in my life, nor did I know by sight any person related to him in any way. After other efforts had been made, I devoted some week, at least, to preparation, and came to Washington, at my own expense, without fee or reward, or the hope of any, in order to press upon the Attorney General and the President those considerations which I deemed proper to be considered in support of the application for executive clemency. The man's life was saved. I never spoke to him until I accompanied Mr. Marshal Freeman to his cell, and assisted in the reading of the President's warrant of commutation. I have sometimes done just such things as that on other occasions. I do not profess to be a particularly benevolent man, but I mention that as an illustration of what I *might* do, even for a stranger.

Question. You have spoken of your opinion that evidence might have been obtained from Boston to Kansas to show that Brown was insane. Will you say whether, as far as you know, it was his general reputation in Massachusetts, that he was insane?

Answer. I cannot answer to that. I took that position in my letter to Judge Blair, in consequence of an inference drawn by myself from circumstances attending the outbreak at Harper's Ferry—the outbreak itself, and the circumstances attending it. It was my own inference. I am not aware that I had ever heard it suggested by any man that Captain Brown was insane. I have since been informed that some twenty-five or thirty affidavits were taken in different parts of the country and submitted to the executive of Virginia, in support of some theory of insanity, in behalf of Captain Brown.

Question. Were you aware that a young gentleman named Hoyt had been sent to Virginia as counsel for Brown and his associates?

Answer. I knew that Mr. Hoyt went to Virginia. I personally know Mr. Hoyt. He is a very young man, a very excellent young man, a gentleman of talent, but inexperienced as a lawyer, and he would not regard himself, nor would he be regarded by others, as a gentleman of that degree of professional experience to be placed in a position of such responsibility as the defence of a capital cause, in a strange State, under foreign laws.

Question. Were you aware or cognizant of who sent him, who employed him to go, at whose instance he went?

Answer. To the extent of my knowledge, I can speak, and I have no doubt that I, substantially, know the facts. I think Mr. Hoyt went without compensation, and I think his expenses, which of course would be small, were paid by gentlemen whom he knew. It is customary with us, as I suppose it is everywhere, for gentlemen of the bar, particularly younger members of the bar, to act as volunteer counsel in capital causes, and even in other important criminal causes, where the parties are not able to procure counsel by compensation. Mr. Hoyt went to Virginia before Mr. Chilton, and when he left Boston I think he had no means of knowing, or suspecting, probably, what I intended to do. He went suddenly, probably upon an impulse. There might have been a little professional aspiration, for aught I know, mingling with his motives.

Question. You have spoken of a custom prevailing at Boston, and probably at the bar generally, for junior members of the bar to volunteer in criminal causes where the party is not able to pay counsel; is it customary for them to volunteer their services to go out of their own State, and to a remote State for that purpose?

Answer. I do not remember any other instance save one, and that occurred in this very case of Brown and his associates, in the person of Mr. Sennott, who is a Democrat, and a supporter of the Democratic federal administration.

Question. What did he do?

Answer. He went in the same way. I think Mr. Sennott had no compensation at all when he went to Virginia—that is, no promise of any, and I do not know that he has ever been paid anything. I do not know whether, in his recent visit to Virginia within a few days past to defend Stevens, Mr. Sennott went as a mere volunteer or upon the promise of compensation; but I am very sure that Mr. Sennott and Mr. Hoyt both went to Virginia originally, without any expectation of pecuniary compensation.

Question. How did you derive that information?

Answer. I am very sure that both Mr. Hoyt and Mr. Sennott told me so. It was a case of a great deal of public impression, as you perceive, and it is not very strange that young men might perceive, or think they perceived in it, an opportunity for some exercise of professional prowess, and that, added to a sentiment of humanity or pity for a man deemed to be in circumstances of hardship and misfortune, would be a sufficient motive to operate on many minds.

Question. Will you inform the committee whether, at any time during the years 1858 or 1859, you contributed money in any form to be paid over to John Brown for any purpose? I mean before the Harper's Ferry affair.

Answer. I never saw Mr. Brown until some time in the spring of 1859. I never contributed any money in aid of any purposes of Mr. Brown's whatsoever, unless contributions which I may have made to the Emigrant Aid Society or to the Kansas committee may have indirectly reached him, of which last fact I am, however, wholly without any means of information. But after having met Captain Brown one Sunday evening at a lady's house, where I made a social call with my wife, I sent to him $25 as a present.

Question. Was that in the spring of 1859?

Answer. Yes, sir. I do not know the date, but it was sometime in the spring of 1859. I do not know whether anybody else gave him any money or not. I sent him $25. I did it because I felt ashamed, after I had seen the old man and talked with him, and come within the reach of the personal impression, (which I find he very generally made on people), that I had never contributed anything directly towards his assistance, as one whom I thought had sacrificed and suffered so much for the cause of freedom and of good order and good government in the Territory of Kansas. He was, if I may be allowed to use that expression, a very magnetic person, and I felt very much impressed by him. I confess I did not know how to understand the old gentleman fully, because when I hear a man talk upon great themes, touching which I think he must have deep feeling, in a tone perfectly level, without emphasis and without any exhibition of feeling, I am always ready to suspect that there is something wrong in the man's brain.

I noticed that the old gentleman in conversation scarcely regarded other people, was entirely self-poised, self-possessed, sufficient to himself, and appeared to have no emotion of any sort, but to be entirely absorbed in an idea, which pre-occupied him and seemed to put him in a position transcending an ordinary emotion and ordinary reason. I did not regard him as a dangerous man, however. I thought that his sufferings and hardships and bereavements had produced some effect upon him. I sent him $25, and in parting with him, as I heard he was a poor man, I expressed my gratitude to him for having fought for a great cause with earnestness, fidelity, and conscientiousness, while I had been quietly at home earning my money and supporting my family in Boston under my own vine and fig tree, with nobody to make me afraid.

By Mr. Doolittle:

Question. Was the whole amount of money you paid refunded to you, or how much were you left out of pocket?

Answer. I have not carefully examined, for I came to Washington without having any information as to the point towards which the examination of the committee would tend. I have not examined my accounts. Perhaps I am out of pocket $100. If I do not lose more than $50 or $100, besides conducting the correspondence, I am satisfied.

By Mr. Davis:

Question.—You state that your sympathy with Brown arose from the useful service rendered by him in Kansas for the preservation of good order and government. Will you state what the character of the service was which you so denominate?

Answer. At a time when, according to the best and all the information which I possessed, there was no law, nor official of the law, to protect, or who did protect, the free-State settlers from Massachusetts and from the South, too, I am led to believe that Mr. Brown was efficient, with other men, in the attempt to guard and protect and secure them against unlawful violence from marauders, resident or pretending to be resident in Kansas, and invaders from adjoining slaveholding States.

Question. Did you include in those services what is known as the Pottawatomie murders?

Answer. No, sir; for I have always understood that Captain Brown was not present at the Pottawatomie transaction. I, however, have heard that Captain Brown said that he approved the transaction at Pottawatomie as an action of necessary self-defence, though he was not himself personally present. I was never in Kansas in my life, and am dependent wholly for my opinions on those who have visited Kansas, and who have given me information.

Question. There was another feat of his, that of kidnapping negroes in Missouri, and running them off to Iowa. Was that a part of his services which commanded your sympathy?

Answer. The transaction to which you refer is one which I do not, from my point of view, regard as justifiable. I suppose Captain Brown did, and I presume I should not judge him severely at all for that transaction, because I should suppose that he might have regarded that, if not defensive, at least offensive warfare in the nature of defence—an aggression to prevent or repel aggressions. And I think that his foray into Virginia was a fruit of the Kansas tree. I think that he and his associates had been educated up to the point of making an unlawful, and even unjustifiable, attack upon the people of a neighboring State—had been taught to do so, and educated to do so by the attacks which the free State men in Kansas suffered from people of the slaveholding States. And, since the gentleman has called my attention again to that subject, I think the attack which was made against representative government in the assault upon Senator Sumner in Washington, which, so far as I could learn from the public press, was, if not justified, at least winked at throughout the South, was an act of very much greater danger to our liberties and to civil society than the attack of a few men upon neighbors over the borders of a State. I suppose that, the State of Virginia is wealthy and strong, and brave enough to defend itself against the assaults of any unorganized unlawful force.

Mr. Davis. My purpose is to learn whether the witness and those who aided in their contributions had their sympathy for Brown excited by deeds of murder and robbery, or whether those acts did not diminish their sympathy.

The Witness. I think I ought to say in reply, that I was not aware that I ever heard of the Pottawatomie transaction until since Captain Brown's trial. Therefore, the Pottawatomie transaction could not have affected my mind at all either way. I have not been accustomed to discriminate much between one and another of the Kansas conflicts. They were general, and there were many of them. I had heard of the Ossawatomie affair, but I do not remember to have heard about the transaction at Pottawatomie. I undoubtedly had read of it because I read the report of the investigating committee in 1856. It, however, had passed out of my mind, and I remember that in the affidavits taken by Mr Oliver on that committee there was but one man who professed to identify Captain Brown as connected with that transaction, and I am not sure that he expressed himself with certainty.

Question. Had you heard of his stealing horses, to be taken into Ohio and sold?

Answer. I had heard it frequently said that, sometime during the controversy between the Free State men and the pro-slavery men, they were accustomed, when they prevailed against each other, to treat their horses as fairly the spoils of war. I am quite confident that I had heard this statement made in connection with Captain Brown, but I did not regard him singular in that respect, and I always believed and do now believe that the Free State men were acting defensively in substantially all that was done by them in Kansas.

Mr. Davis. Then it was sympathy for a soldier engaged in such a war as you have described?

The Witness. Your question is incomplete, Mr. Davis.

Mr. Davis. I will give it any form which will enable you to answer it more satisfactorily to yourself.

The Witness. You said it was sympathy—

Mr. Davis. The sympathy which you say you expressed or felt towards John Brown, is that which you felt for a soldier engaged in such a civil war as that which you describe in Kansas.

The Witness. That would hardly be a fair statement of my feeling.

Mr. Davis. I wish merely to get what your feeling is. It is not a statement, but an inquiry.

The Witness. I am constitutionally peaceable, and by opinion very much of a peace man, and I have very little faith in deeds of violence, and very little sympathy with them except as the extremest and direst necessity. My sympathy, so far as I sympathized with Captain Brown was on account of what I believed to be heroic and disinterested services in defence of a good and just cause, and in support of the rights of persons who were treated with unjust aggression.

By Mr. Fitch:

Question. There is a question which, perhaps, would be germane. Without saying to the witness what has, or what has not been in proof heretofore before the committee, we could put this supposition to him: suppose that it had been known that Brown had had in contemplation precisely such a thing as he was guilty of in Virginia, for fifteen or twenty years; that he sought this Kansas service for the very purpose of educating himself and those who acted with him for this ulterior object, would the witness and those who sympathized with him, have sympathized with his Kansas operations, with that knowledge.

Answer. I have no reason to suspect that of myself, nor do I believe of any other gentleman with whom I agree or not, that the transactions of Captain Brown at Harper's Ferry would be deemed justifiable, nor would any such attempt made or contemplated, receive our sympathy.

Mr. Fitch. The answer does not go to the full extent desired. I intended to ascertain from the witness, whether, if he and those who acted with him, had supposed that Brown had contemplated this Harper's Ferry foray, using the means, and men they were placing at his disposal in Kansas for that purpose, they would have given him those means, or encouraged him in his Kansas operations?

The Witness. Of course not. So far as a man can answer hypothetically, I say, of course not.

By Mr. Davis:

Question. You stated when you first saw Brown; will you state when you last saw him?

Answer. I never saw him but once, and I thought it singular that I should not have seen him, for I heard he was frequently in Boston. I was not a member of the Kansas committee or any Kansas association.

Question. Do you know when he was last in Boston?

Answer. I have never heard that Mr. Brown was in Boston since the time when I saw him, last spring. He may have been there, though.

By Mr. Collamer:

Question. In the Pottawatomie transaction which has been spoken of, as you understood the thing, did you understand that Mr. Brown was participating in it?

Answer. I will say that I never did believe, and from the best information I have ever received, I do not now believe, that Captain Brown was present, and a participator in the transaction. It would be fair for me to say, I think, with regard to other gentlemen who may have contributed towards this money, that I ought not, perhaps, to be taken as a representative of them all, because I may be a very much more ultra man in my opinions than they. I think there were Democrats who contributed towards that money, though I have not a personal knowledge of the fact. The money was handed towards my fund merely for the purpose of securing a fair trial. I am confident that some people gave under the impression that it would be better for the peace of the country to have it more apparent that Captain Brown was well defended.

JOHN A. ANDREW.

Letter from John A. Andrew.

BOSTON, July 31st, 1860.

MY DEAR SIR—I shall not be able to regulate my engagements so as to attend the celebration at Abington of "The Anniversary of British West Indian Emancipation," to which you have invited me.

I should be glad if it were in my power to add emphasis to my declaration of faith in the *wisdom*, as well as the *benevolence* which compelled the Christian people of Great Britain to demand that great measure of justice from their government. It is, in my judgment, beyond reasonable doubt, that sound political economy, as well as national security and tranquility, requires that the people who inhabit every country shall be free to enjoy their natural rights. The argument which would enslave the negroes and mulattoes of the West Indies, is equally good in kind, if not equally forcible in degree, to justify the maintenance of servitude in Russia, and the degradation of many white populations in Europe; and indeed I am well satisfied that nothing but the existence of universal suffrage in the United States (for white men) prevents the frank advocacy of the principle of the ownership of labor by capital in reference to the free *white* laborers in our own country. Had not the ballot-box, open to every citizen, and the school house, open to every citizen's child, and the public press, free to declare itself concerning every subject, established their authority so firmly among us, I have no doubt that slavery would be argued by some men in New York and New England to be the proper condition for our laboring classes.

Had the theories of many distinguished men, now prevalent, been the doctrines of those who shaped our institutions during the last quarter of the last century, there would, I verily believe, have been a "Dred Scott decision" for whites as well as for blacks.

I do not regard the question of "negro emancipation" precisely as you do. It is not, in any sense, a sectional question. So far as the controversy concerning it is now in a sectional form, it is only accidentally and temporarily so. It needs nothing now but a just and honest administration of the National Government to develope throughout the whole South a sentiment of opposition to the perpetuation of slavery.

At present, few Southern men dare, and fewer still are able, to withstand the combination of their State and Federal Governments in the interest of a single class of capitalists. The controversy will not only soon cease to have a sectional form, but it will cease even to be *called* sectional. It will be recognized in its real proportions as a *universal* question,—not sectional, nor even national, but universal, touching the rights not of a class only, nor of a race, but of the whole human family.

Into whose souls, even now, does the iron of slavery in America enter with the bitterest pain and the deepest wound? Not into those of black men who never knew liberty scarcely so much as even by name, either in their own persons or in those of their fathers; but into those of the free, white, native-born Americans to whom it is not permitted, under pain of insult, fine, imprisonment, and even of death, to read the speeches and books of men born and educated at the South like themselves, appealing to the patriotism and the interest of the South against the doctrines of the propagators of slavery.

Powerful men, in large numbers, hold black men and oppress white ones in the fifteen slaveholding States. Powerful men, in large numbers, in the eighteen free States, are equally insensible to the rights and wrongs of these white and black men. They affect to treat with indifference the rights of labor everywhere, and the wrongs which it suffers now at the hands of the nation, and with the aggravation of which it is threatened for the future.

If Slavery, emboldened by the "Dred Scott decision," shall by means of the "Lemmon case," be decreed a foothold as a sojourning institution in all the free States; and,—by means of the Breckinridge *audacity*, the Douglas *indifference*, and the Bell and Everett *ignor-ance* policies,—gain a new lease of National power—the necessarily consequent restoration of the foreign trade in negro slaves, and the cheapening of human cattle, will at last teach the dumbest tongue to cry out, the coldest heart to feel, and the blindest incarnation of respectable nonchalance to see, that the only remaining inquiry for the American people is, *Whether all poor men shall be slaves, or all slaves shall be made free* ?

With more particular regard to your invitation to me to be present on Wednesday at Abington, perhaps it is due to a perfectly frank understanding that I should say, (what I believe you already know,) that though I am with you and your friends in sympathy when you rejoice that the British slave is now a free man, yet I have been so often pained at the unremitting and I think frequently unjust assaults by persons upon your platform on men whom I greatly respect, and whose services in the cause of rational and impartial liberty I highly prize, that I could not fail to esteem myself an intruder in your midst — unless I should suppress something I might feel urged to say. My fidelity to the existing institution of Government, its charters, its organization, and the duties of its citizenship, is, ever has been, and, I doubt not, will always be, unshaken; but, working in the sphere of citizenship, and through the instrumentalities it affords, I hope that I ever may remember the lesson of British Emancipation, and apply it wherever I have the right and the power.

Yours, respectfully and faithfully,

JOHN A. ANDREW.

TO MR. GARRISON.

From the Boston Traveller.

John Brown and John A. Andrew.

The organ of the "Constitutional Union Party" assails Mr. Andrew, the Republican candidate for Governor, in very violent style. We give a few specimens of its manner of conducting the war against this gentleman:

"We shall also ask our readers to recall the history of John Brown's exploits, which the Republican candidate tells us were *right*. 'A citizen of one of the Northern States of this Union, at the head of other citizens, on a certain Lord's day,—on that day of holy rest—entered armed—armed for murder and treason—into the State of Virginia; burst open the houses of private citizens, and seized them and their property by force, and slaughtered in the streets inoffensive, unarmed men.' Mr. John A. Andrew says this was *right*."

"There are those who characterize John Brown's murders at Harper's Ferry, as 'God's work.' Mr. John A. Andrew and Mr. Dwight Foster, we dare say, think there was something divine in the bloody deeds done in that unsuspecting Virginia village, on that Sabbath morning, October 16, 1859."

[Here follows a recapitulation of Brown's exploits, and then the Courier continues]:

"Here we have a record of five men murdered at Harper's Ferry, by John Brown; and Mr. John A. Andrew, the Republican candidate for Governor, tells you the *murderer was right*."

Yesterday's issue brought out the following:

"If the thousands of business men of Boston, who signed the call for a Union meeting, in Faneuil Hall, in December last, were in earnest—if the many more thousands of Massachusetts men who publicly responded to that call were sincere in their opposition to *the atrocious doctrines and action of John Brown, which were deliberately endorsed by John A. Andrew*—this is the time and occasion for action."

And after another summary of Brown's actions we are told that—

"These are the deeds of blood, unexampled in this country, among a peaceful community, *which the Abolitionists of Massachusetts, by their action of last Wednesday, tell us were right*, and call upon our citizens to sustain and to approve by a deliberate vote."

Then follows an appeal to the people to unite in the prayer that no such spectacle of horror shall be again witnessed. And, adds the Courier:

"That it may not be, let no such record ever be made that those men are elected to the chief offices of Massachusetts *who supplied John Brown with the weapons of midnight murder*, and afterwards mourned over him, and, directly or indirectly, celebrated the memory of his crimes!"

These quotations, which we have picked out of a mass of similar highly seasoned reading, not only charge Mr. Andrew with approving of John Brown's foray, but, substantially, with furnishing him with the weapons of his midnight murder! We should be loath to think that this language and this mode of assailing Mr. Andrew are approved by one, at least, of the editors of the Courier, and still more loath to believe that the "conservative republicans" to whom that paper appeals could be influenced by such frantic, extravagant and one-sided language. The simple truth is that Mr. Andrew not only did not furnish weapons and money for the Harper's Ferry Invasion, and did not approve of that invasion; but that he expressly and in the plainest terms, in his testimony before the Senatorial Committee, stated his entire disapprobation of the enterprise. Mr. Andrew's position as indicated in his testimony, and in his speech at the Tremont Temple, needs no explanation or apology; it only needs to be made known. It would be well for the Courier to recollect that it is two months before the election, and that our Massachusetts people are not in the habit of making up their minds in a hurry, when they have plenty of time for examination and thought. Its attempt to entrap voters into a hasty condemnation of Mr. Andrew by such unscrupulous means as those we have noted, will certainly fail. The great mass of the supporters of Bell and Everett, and of the "conservative Republicans," who, it is hoped, may be influenced by these appeals, are intelligent and honest men, who will not only deal fairly with all candidates presented for their suffrages, but who will surely disapprove all attempts to forestall public opinion by unfair means.

This is what Mr. Andrew *did* in relation to John Brown:—

He presided at a meeting held at the Tremont Temple for the relief of the family of Brown; a meeting at which Rev. Dr. Rollin H. Neale offered prayer, and Rev. Mr. Manning, Ralph Waldo Emerson, and Wendell Phillips spoke.

He employed Mr. Chilton of Washington, and Mr. Green of Richmond, to defend Brown in the Charlestown Court, and present his case before the Court of Errors; guaranteeing to them $1300 as fees, and raising the money by the aid of friends and by his own exertions.

What he *said* may be found at length in the Harper's Ferry Report, and in the report of the John Brown meeting. In his evidence before the Senatorial Committee he states with admirable frankness not only his proceedings in behalf of Brown, but the motives which governed him, viz: sympathy for a man who had done good service in Kansas, and a desire that "a judicial outrage" should not be perpetrated by hurrying him to trial without affording him a fair chance for a defence. If he had supposed that Brown and his associates were in the way of having a fair trial, he would not have interfered, for he says "I had no sympathy with his peculiar conduct touching which he was then indicted. I felt injured by that, personaly, as a Republican." Nay, more; when asked by Mr. Fitch if he would have sympathized with Brown's Kansas operations if he had known or supposed that he sought service in that territory for the purpose of educating himself for the Harper's Ferry work, Mr. Andrew replied:

"I have no reason to suspect that of myself, nor do I believe of any other gentleman with whom I agree or act, that the transactions of Capt. Brown at Harper's Ferry would be deemed justifiable, nor would any such attempt, made or contemplated, receive our sympathy."

When asked his opinion of Brown's feat of "kidnapping negroes in Missouri and running them off into Iowa," Mr. Andrew replied:—

"The transaction to which you refer is one which I do not, from my point of view, regard as justifiable. I suppose Capt. Brown did; and I presume I should not judge him severely at all for that transaction, because I should suppose that he might have regarded that, if not defensive, at least offensive warfare in the nature of defence—an aggression to prevent or repel aggression."

He goes on to trace Brown's invasion to the events in Kansas, and to compare it with the assault on Mr. Sumner, which he considered "an act of very much greater danger to our liberties and to civil society than the attack of a few men upon neighbors over the borders of a State."

Such being the opinions and the acts of Mr. Andrew, in this connection, it is easy to understand what he meant when he said at the Tremont Temple—

"I pause not to consider, because it is wholly outside of the duty or the thought of this assembly to-night, whether the enterprise of John Brown and his associates in Virginia was wise or foolish, right or wrong. I know only that whether the enterprise itself was the one or the other, JOHN BROWN HIMSELF IS RIGHT."

Not "was" right, as the Courier mischievously prints it; but "*is*" right. And who disputes it? Who does not remember that the people of Massachusetts, without regard to party, or age, or sex, or condition, saving and excepting only a few men of the extreme pro-slavery school, who would disapprove of even Divine interposition against the institution which, in their opinion, is the bond of our Union, the palladium of our liberties, and the safeguard and sure defence of our religion; who does not remember that the people were stirred to an unwonted degree of emotion and sympathy by the gallant and fruitless attempt of Brown and his handful of associates to carry to the oppressed black people of Virginia that freedom which is the birthright of all men? Who has forgotten that patient and heroic man, an enthusiast and a fanatic, but not a felon, and only by the harshest misuse of terms a "murderer," risking his life for the realization of an idea; extorting the admiration of even Henry A. Wise by his manly bearing, and taming the ferocity of a Virginia populace by his calmness and dignity; standing at bay; not seeking blood, but avoiding it, and, by avoiding it, entangling himself in the meshes of the net and allowing himself to be captured; writing to his friends letters full of sublime and Christian thoughts, and going to the scaffold as resignedly as common men go to their beds? Are we expected in our zeal for slavery-extension, or in our indifference towards it, to smother all the instincts of our human nature, and to join in an outcry against such a man as if he was a highwayman, a seducer, a pirate, a midnight assassin? Is a respectable, philanthropic gentleman who is presented as a candidate for office by a great party, to be pounced upon, off-hand, and maligned after the fashion of the articles from which we have quoted, and held up to public abhorrence because he has felt as other men felt, and while regretting and disapproving Brown's acts, honored him for his heroism and sympathised with his sufferings. We are yet not quite ready to believe it.

One word more. We respectfully suggest to the conservative citizens of Boston that the policy of representing to the people of the South that the party which has nominated Mr. Andrew, and which will surely elect him, is a party which approves of murder and pillage and border warfare, is a very questionable one, to say the least, for our material interests. We put it to the merchants of Boston, in all seriousness, whether such representations as to the hostile intentions of a great number of our citizens, are well calculated to restore harmony between the North and the South, or to advance in any essential degree our business interests. It strikes us that this is a matter worth thinking of.

THE REPUBLICAN PLATFORM.

Resolved, That we, the delegated representatives of the Republican electors of the United States, in convention assembled, in discharge of the duty we owe to our constituents and our country, unite in the following declarations:—

1. That the history of the nation, during the last four years, has fully established the propriety and necessity of the organization and perpetuation of the Republican party, and that the causes which called it into existence are permanent in their nature, and now, more than ever before, demand its peaceful and constitutional triumph.

2. That the maintenance of the principles promulgated in the Declaration of Independence, and embodied in our Federal Constitution, that "all men are created equal; that they are endowed by their Creator with certain unalienable rights; that among these are life, liberty, and the pursuit of happiness; that to secure these rights governments are instituted among men, deriving their just powers from the consent of the governed," is essential to the preservation of our Republican institutions; and that the Federal Constitution, the rights of the States, and the Union of the States must and shall be preserved.

3 That to the Union of the States this nation owes its unprecedented increase in population, its surprising development of material resources, its rapid augmentation of wealth, its happiness at home and its honor abroad; and we hold in abhorrence all schemes for disunion, come from whatever source they may; and we congratulate the country that no Republican member of Congress has uttered or countenanced the threats of disunion, so often made by Democratic members, without rebuke and with applause from their political associates; and we denounce those threats of disunion, in case of a popular overthrow of their ascendency, as denying the vital principles of a free government, and as an avowal of contemplated treason, which it is the imperative duty of an indignant people strongly to rebuke and forever silence.

4. That the maintenance inviolate of the rights of the States, and especially the right of each State to order and control its own domestic institutions, according to its own judgment exclusively, is essential to that balance of power on which the perfection and endurance of our political faith depend; and we denounce the lawless invasion by armed force of any State or Territory, no matter under what pretext, as among the gravest of crimes.

5. That the present Democratic administration has far exceeded our worst apprehensions, in its measureless subserviency to the exactions of a sectional interest, as especially evinced in its desperate exertions to force the infamous Lecompton Constitution upon the protesting people of Kansas; in construing the personal relation between master and servant, to involve an unqualified property in persons; in its attempted enforcement everywhere, on land and sea, through the intervention of Congress and the federal courts, of the extreme pretensions of a purely local interest; and in its general and unvarying abuse of the power intrusted to it by a confiding people.

6. That the people justly view with alarm the reckless extravagance which pervades every department of the federal government; that a return to rigid economy and accountability is indispensable to arrest the systematic plunder of the public treasury by favored partisans; while the recent startling developments of frauds and corruptions at the federal metropolis show that an entire change of administration is imperatively demanded.

7. That the new dogma that the Constitution of its own force carries slavery into any or all the territories of the United States, is a dangerous political heresy, at variance with the explicit provisions of that instrument itself, with contemporaneous exposition, and with legislative and judicial precedent; is revolutionary in its tendency, and subversive of the peace and harmony of the country.

8. That the normal condition of all the territory of the United States is that of freedom; that as our republican fathers, when they had abolished slavery in all our national territory, ordained that "no person should be deprived of life, liberty, or property, without due process of law," it becomes our duty, by legislation, whenever legislation is necessary, to maintain this provision of the Constitution against all attempts to violate it; and we deny the authority of Congress, of a territorial legislature, or of any individuals, to give legal existence to slavery in any territory of the United States.

9. That we brand the recent reopening of the African slave trade, under the cover of our national flag, aided by perversions of judicial power, as a crime against humanity and a burning shame to our country and age; and we call upon Congress to take prompt and efficient measures for the total and final suppression of that execrable traffic.

10. That in the recent vetoes by their federal governors of the acts of the Legislatures of Kansas and Nebraska, prohibiting slavery in those territories, we find a practical illustration of the boasted democratic principle of non-intervention and popular sovereignty, embodied in the Kansas and Nebraska bill, and a demonstration of the deception and fraud involved therein.

11. That Kansas should of right be immediately admitted as a State under the constitution recently formed and adopted by her people, and accepted by the House of Representatives.

12. That while providing revenue for the support of the general government by duties upon imposts, sound policy requires such an adjustment of these imposts as to encourage the development of the industrial interests of the whole country; and we commend that policy of national exchanges which secures to the workingmen liberal wages; to agriculture remunerating prices; to mechanics and manufacturers an adequate reward for their skill, labor, and enterprise; and to the nation commercial prosperity and independence.

13. That we protest against any sale or alienation to others of the public lands held by actual settlers, and against any view of the homestead policy, which regards the settlers as paupers or supplicants for public bounty; and we demand the passage by Congress of the complete and satisfactory homestead measure which has already passed the House.

14. That the Republican party is opposed to any change in our naturalization laws, or any State legislation by which the rights of citizenship, hitherto accorded to immigrants from foreign lands, shall be abridged or impaired; and in favor of giving a full and efficient protection to the rights of all classes of citizens, whether native or naturalized, both at home and abroad.

15. That appropriations by Congress for river and harbor improvements of a national character, required for the accommodation and security of an existing commerce, are authorized by the Constitution, and justified by the obligation of Government to protect the lives and property of its citizens.

16. That a railroad to the Pacific Ocean is imperatively demanded by the interests of the whole country; that the federal government ought to render immediate and efficient aid in its construction; and that, as preliminary thereto, a daily overland mail should be promptly established.

17. Finally, having thus set forth our distinctive principles and views, we invite the co-operation of all citizens, however differing on other questions, who substantially agree with us in their affirmance and support.

The following is the reply of John A. Andrew to an invitation to be present at the Myrick's Grove Republican mass meeting, on the 18th inst.:—

"BOSTON, Sept 6, 1860.

To Messrs. Jonathan Bourne, Jr., E. Thornton, Jr., Warren Ladd, and other Republicans of New Bedford.

Gentlemen:—Without a moment's delay I hasten to accept your invitation. I cannot hope to add anything to the stock of ideas on political affairs common to all, by any public declaration of my individual sentiments. But your wish, coming from so many gentlemen, for whose persons and characters I have a respect which entitles them to command me, must in this instance be my law. I had hoped earnestly that I might not appear in person on the field during the progress of our present State canvass. The opinions of wiser men differ from my desire, and I shall not shrink out of sentiments of merely personal delicacy flowing from my own relations to the canvass, from the performance of this duty which is thought to be due to the cause.

There is but little disunionism anywhere, even in the South, besides that which is stimulated by Northern speculators in national politics practicing on Southern apprehensions, and systematically misleading Southern minds. The South can take care of its own disunionism. There are Southern men enough to drive that monster into the Gulf of Mexico without a Northern man or gun. And if need be, they would do it.

The real danger is not to the *Union* but to the *people*. Let *all* the people *agree* that they will seek to understand all questions entering into our public affairs, determine that they will meet them, discuss and decide them, dismiss their self-constituted guardians, and banish the prophets of evil, the Balaams of our Israel—and all will be well.

If we of the North are to be frightened by the question of slavery, in what a condition must they be who in the South are watching for the dawn of Freedom's day; when slave masters and free laborers may unite to lift the heaviest bond, which white as well as black men ever bore?

With great respect and regard,

I am faithfully yours,

(Signed) JOHN A. ANDREW."

www.ingramcontent.com/pod-product-compliance
Lightning Source LLC
LaVergne TN
LVHW020644110826
845149LV00004B/1345

* 9 7 8 1 4 1 8 1 9 0 1 5 6 *